A New Resonance

9

Emerging Voices
in
English-Language
Haiku

Edited by Jim Kacian & Dee Evetts

A New Resonance 9:
  Emerging Voices in English-Language Haiku

© 2015 by Jim Kacian
for Red Moon Press
All Rights Reserved

First Printing

Published by
Red Moon Press
PO Box 2461
Winchester VA
22604-1661 USA
www.redmoonpress.com

ISBN 978-1-936848-42-3

All work published with permission of the individual authors or their accredited agents.

Cover Painting:
John Twachtman, *Brook Among the Trees* (1891)
Pastel; 25.72 x 23.81 cm.
Private collection.
Used with permission.

Foreword

It's fair to say that the mission for the New Resonance series has changed over time. What began simply as a showcase for rising talent has evolved into something considerably more. We now see New Resonance as a place where a poet of any pedigree and prior success might successfully exhibit a substantial amount of work in a single venue, still a remarkably rare event in the haiku world. And while we still maintain that this is one step toward recognition on a larger scale, and hence the adjective "emerging" still obtains, we also recognize that an even more palpable effect of this recognition is the creation of a highly specific community, the New Resonance community, the members of which will nearly all go on to publish their own books and have a larger forum for their work and ideas. But they will have started here, and that will be a fact that will gather them together in their own minds and in ours. Given that we've already conducted one memorable New Resonance reading (at Haiku North America 2009) and are planning others, there's good reason to think that this community will have a collective force in the growth and development of English-language haiku, and, based on the high quality of the work you'll find in these pages, that our genre has a very bright future.

Jim Kacian & Dee Evetts
Series Editors

A New Resonance

9

Stewart Baker

Brad Bennett

Claire Everett

Kate S. Godsey

Cara Holman

P M F Johnson

Gregory Longenecker

Jonathan McKeown

Ben Moeller-Gaa

Beverly Acuff Momoi

Polona Oblak

Thomas Powell

Brendan Slater

William Sorlien

Michelle Tennison

Scott Terrill

Julie Warther

Stewart C. Baker

Academic Librarian

Born 3 July 1982
Croydon, England
Currently Resides
Dallas, Oregon

If the early part of our adulthood is largely consumed with finding our places in the world, and the late part with preserving what we find, the middle is where the actual work takes place. Extending a relationship beyond infatuation, or learning to let it go, acquiring patience, reading the symbols of the planet and the stars, meeting the challenges of acceptance and resistance, illness and health—these are the circumstances that deepen our character and define it for others. Baker's poems meet these events directly, in a clean style that is alert to the telling word and the necessary image. We easily trust these words, and believe the larger sense of them which expands within us upon reading.

Credits

all the things	*Frogpond* 36.2
eating away	unpublished
repossessed	unpublished
perihelion	unpublished
geese	unpublished
all week waiting	unpublished
low tide	*Modern Haiku* 45.2
driftwood fire	unpublished
streetlamps	*The Heron's Nest* 16.3
edged	*A Hundred Gourds* 2.2
resounding deep	*Bones* 5
between	*Kokako* 20
ashes	unpublished
hummingbird	*Northwest Passage* 11.3
another talk	*Frogpond* 35.3

"another talk" to appear in *A Vast Sky* (forthcoming, Charles E. Tuttle).

all the things
I said I'd do . . .
winter sunset

eating away
at last year's argument . . .
first fog

repossessed
she ties another poem
to the full moon

perihelion
she doesn't want to talk
about divorce

geese
veering out of heavy fog—
she doesn't call back

all week waiting
for the other shoe to drop . . .
cloudbursts

low tide
captured by my footprints
a tiny crab

driftwood fire she walks into the sunset

streetlamps . . .
the slow migration
of a snail

edged with wildflowers their latest fight for custody

resounding deep within the cat's purr bone cancer

between
your parting words . . .
old-growth forest

ashes the admission of everything past tense

hummingbird . . .
startled by your
absent laughter

another talk
that's only in my head . . .
summer rain

Stewart Baker

Brad Bennett

Claire Everett

Kate S. Godsey

Cara Holman

P M F Johnson

Gregory Longenecker

Jonathan McKeown

Ben Moeller-Gaa

Beverly Acuff Momoi

Polona Oblak

Thomas Powell

Brendan Slater

William Sorlien

Michelle Tennison

Scott Terrill

Julie Warther

Brad Bennett

Elementary School Teacher

Born 1 September 1960
Philadelphia, Pennsylvania
Currently Resides
Arlington, Massachusetts

Bashō, who for many years made his living as a renga master, once described the rarest and best sort of link as a "scent." By this he meant the connection between verses was just a trace, about as far from cause and effect as possible while still maintaining a linkage. Many of Bennett's best poems are "scent" haiku—who would see the inevitability of the relationship between a blue Cadillac and the year's longest day, or squash seeds and New Year's resolutions, until pointed out. These are precisely what the poet notices, and, by sharing them with us, helps us notice. Once seen, they are indeed hard to forget.

Credits

New Year's resolutions	*cattails* 4
steady rain	*Acorn* 32
my feet	*Biting the Sun*
silence	*Frogpond* 35.3
all those tiny holes	*Acorn* 31
the longest day	*tinywords* 14.1
switchbacks	*this world*
our return trip	*bottle rockets* 29
commuting	unpublished
company for lunch	Kaji Aso Contest 2013
end of the line	*Presence* 50
late December	*cattails* 4
quickly	*Modern Haiku* 45.2
waiting	*The Heron's Nest* 13.3
spring	*bottle rockets* 31

"my feet" and "company for lunch" appeared in *Biting the Sun* (Boston Haiku Society, 2014); "switchbacks" appeared in *this world*, The Haiku Society of America Members' Anthology 2013.

New Year's resolutions—
scraping the seeds out
of the butternut

steady rain
a dented sap bucket
by the stone wall

my feet
straddle the sun—
new swing set

silence . . .
a white butterfly stutters
across the meadow

all those tiny holes
in the maple leaves . . .
summer days

the longest day
a sky blue Cadillac
drives slowly by

switchbacks
up the mountain
we swap regrets

our return trip
the landscape painters
further along

commuting
on Monday morning—
the new moon's nothing

company for lunch
a dozen eggs knock
against the pot

end of the line
I wake the subway rider
by nudging his toe

late December
the radiator hiss
ends with a ting

quickly
forgetting
the
first
snow
flake

waiting
becomes living
late winter

spring for a day until one day spring

Stewart Baker

Brad Bennett

Claire Everett

Kate S. Godsey

Cara Holman

P M F Johnson

Gregory Longenecker

Jonathan McKeown

Ben Moeller-Gaa

Beverly Acuff Momoi

Polona Oblak

Thomas Powell

Brendan Slater

William Sorlien

Michelle Tennison

Scott Terrill

Julie Warther

Claire Everett

Poet & Editor

Born 13 January 1965
Donnington, England
Currently resides
Northallerton, England

Emergence may not be the first quality we associate with haiku, yet the process of becoming is universal, and is a feature of many of Everett's poems. Things previously hidden become visible, things potential or nascent are actualized. The prevailing mode is thus one of transition, whether it be the progress of the seasons, the ordering of human relationships, or the passage of generations. At the same time, we find a perception and acknowledgment of these strands being inextricably entwined. All is underpinned by the poet's discerning eye for patterns and shifts in the natural world. The overall effect is one of quiet nostalgia, as we might expect to encounter in an English garden.

Credits

fiddleheads	*A Hundred Gourds* 3.2
first warm day	*Presence* 50
lilac breeze	*Frogpond* 37.3
butterfly dust	*Acorn* 27
my mother's childhood	*Notes from the Gean* 3.1
testing the flat iron	*Blithe Spirit* 22.1
cumulonimbus	*Acorn* 28
swallows turn	*Blithe Spirit* 24.3
nothing left	*Haiku News* December 1, 2010
black ice	*A Hundred Gourds* 3.1
stone cairn	*A Hundred Gourds* 2.4
a good day to die	*Presence* 49
behind the wheel	*A Hundred Gourds* 2.1
year-round strawberries	*A Hundred Gourds* 2.1
chrysanthemum	*Multiverses* 1

"nothing left" also appeared in *Haiku News Anthology* (ed. Lawrence and Gibson, 2012).

fiddleheads uncoiling all the time in the world

first warm day
a little more crow
in every caw

lilac breeze . . .
the scaffolder straightens
his back

butterfly dust . . .
the question I never
dared to ask

my mother's childhood . . .
from the flower press
a celandine

testing the flat iron . . .
briefly, the weight of
Grandma's days

cumulonimbus
the egret preens deeper
into its breast

swallows turn
back on themselves
gathering dusk

nothing left
but the wishbone . . .
November sky

black ice
and I have no stick—
Heaney is dead

stone cairn—
leaving the past
where it belongs

a good day to die
you say . . .
swifts in the blue

behind the wheel
of a dream I can't drive
perigee moon

year-round strawberries . . .
I've begun to miss
missing you

chrysanthemum unpetalling the scent of rain

Stewart Baker

Brad Bennett

Claire Everett

Kate S. Godsey

Cara Holman

P M F Johnson

Gregory Longenecker

Jonathan McKeown

Ben Moeller-Gaa

Beverly Acuff Momoi

Polona Oblak

Thomas Powell

Brendan Slater

William Sorlien

Michelle Tennison

Scott Terrill

Julie Warther

Kate S. Godsey

Psychotherapist

Born 10 December 1959
Eglan Air Force Base, Florida
Currently Resides
Pacifica, California

Godsey has taken upon herself the same challenge as René Descartes nearly four centuries ago, and for the same reason—a deep questioning of a once-sustaining faith. She takes as a starting point only her belief in her own mind's reality, and reasons outward from there. It is slow and often enigmatic work, and it raises more questions than it provides answers. And yet, slowly, inexorably, borne upon a trust she finds in the natural world's resilience and her own memory, she finds her way back into the whole world, perhaps even, like Descartes, one that is all the larger for the journey.

Credits

death of a child	unpublished
waiting	*bottle rockets* 26
islands of light	*Whirligig* 2.2
perception	unpublished
stealth of raccoons	*World Haiku Review* 2012
milk thistle glistens	unpublished
oklahoma	unpublished
resonance	unpublished
apple blossoms	*A Hundred Gourds* 2.2
jumping off swings	*bottle rockets* 29
smoke rings	*Modern Haiku* 44.3
impossible now	*bottle rockets* 29
low tide	*Frogpond* 35.3
call to prayer	*Modern Haiku* 45.3
all day	unpublished

xxx

death of a child
suddenly these tides
explain everything

waiting
for the other shoe
blue rain

islands of light
on a vast gray sea
how much time is left

perception
the auto-functions
i can't unlock

stealth of raccoons
the intimacy of
a shared solitude

milk thistle glistens
who am i
without mirrors

oklahoma
cutting lavender
in our church shoes

resonance
a rabbit's hole
for Alice

apple blossoms
the easy forgiveness
of children

jumping off swings
the blue that goes on
forever

smoke rings
the lies we tell
our children

impossible now
to pity myself
morning chickadee

low tide
space where the ache
used to be

call to prayer
the song of one bird
rises above the others

all day
sensing plums ripen
it's you, again

Stewart Baker

Brad Bennett

Claire Eaverett

Kate S. Godsey

Cara Holman

P M F Johnson

Gregory Longenecker

Jonathan McKeown

Ben Moeller-Gaa

Beverly Acuff Momoi

Polona Oblak

Thomas Powell

Brendan Slater

William Sorlien

Michelle Tennison

Scott Terrill

Julie Warther

Cara Holman

Math/Reading Specialist

Born 23 July 1957
San Francisco, California
Currently Resides
Portland, Oregon

In this selection from Holman's work we frequently encounter two levels of meaning: the literal and the metaphorical. Far from feeling contrived or becoming formulaic, there is a convincing freshness in the juxtapositions presented. The slow ripening of fruit, the iridescence of an insect's wing, the astringency of pickled plum—these perceptions lend vividness and veracity to the events or emotions they accompany, whether it be a patient waiting, the resolution to some dilemma, or the utterance of words hitherto unvoiced. The range exhibited, from carefree to bleak, provides a context wherein the entire sequence is deepened.

Credits

daydreaming	*Notes from the Gean* 3:1
hide and go seek	*NaHaiWriMo* April 2011
sudden downpour	*Riverwind* 30
greenpeaches	*Frogpond* 34:3
secrets	*Sketchbook* 6:3
dragonfly shimmer	unpublished
morning fog	*Frogpond* 34:3
cancer clinic	*LYNX* 27:3
pickled plum	*Frogpond* 35:3
we promise	unpublished
he asks if it's	*Notes from the Gean* 3:4
hospice ward	HaikuNow! 2012
deepening rain	*LYNX* 27:3
frost footprints	*Notes from the Gean* 3:4
the waiter asks	*Sketchbook Kukai* 5:6

"daydreaming" was included in 2012 Turtle Light Press Competition Favorite Haiku Poems; "secrets" was selected Editor's Choice for *Sketchbook* 6:3; "hospice ward" won 1st place in the Contemporary Category of the 2012 Haiku Now! International Haiku Contest, and also appeared in *Nothing in the Window: The Red Moon Anthology of English-Language Haiku* 2012; "the waiter asks" won 1st place in the Sketchbook Kukai for November/December 2010.

daydreaming
thistledown drifts
on the breeze

hide and go seek
following
the robin's song

sudden downpour
for a moment
I lose my path

green peaches
he says we'll know
when it's time

secrets . . .
the whisper of corn silk
between my fingers

dragonfly shimmer
no decision
becomes my decision

morning fog
one foot
in front of the other

cancer clinic
I silence my cell phone

pickled plum
words I said
I'd never say

we promise
to stay in touch
snow light

he asks if it's
the end of the line
winter moon

hospice ward
the click of the door
behind me

deepening rain
waiting for feeling
to return

frost footprints
my memory of her
fading

the waiter asks
if I'm alone—
winter clouds

Stewart Baker

Brad Bennett

Claire Everett

Kate S. Godsey

Cara Holman

P M F Johnson

Gregory Longenecker

Jonathan McKeown

Ben Moeller-Gaa

Beverly Acuff Momoi

Polona Oblak

Thomas Powell

Brendan Slater

William Sorlien

Michelle Tennison

Scott Terrill

Julie Warther

P M F Johnson

Novelist

Born 4 July 1959
Eden Prairie, Minnesota
Currently Resides
Minneapolis, Minnesota

The fine line to be found between morbid humor and grim desperation is a literary mainstay, but rarely in haiku. Perhaps navigating the thin difference with so few words at our disposal is too daunting, but Johnson's sensibility seems peculiarly attuned to just such distinctions. These poems range from trenchant aperçu to spry self-realization, and are shot through with a keen sense of loss, all without forgoing their balance or sense of scale. The feeling is that the presence behind these poems is a survivor, one who may not win the war, but will not be defeated by it, or fail to find in it its underlying farce.

Credits

Ash Wednesday	*Modern Haiku* 38.3
our father	*Mayfly* 49
even the arms	*Frogpond* 31.3
photo of a man	*Mayfly* 44
unable to remember	*Frogpond* 37.1
the war	*Modern Haiku* 37.1
closing my journal	*Mayfly* 45
the garden	*Frogpond* 35.3
loan	*Modern Haiku* 37.2
after she leaves	*Acorn* 20
this familiar church	*Mayfly* 41
curve of the river	*Frogpond* 37.2
no sex	*Modern Haiku* 38.1
coyote howling	*Acorn* 29
yard gate closed	*Wisteria* 11

"the war" also appeared in *Big Sky: The Red Moon Anthology of English-Language Haiku* 2006 and *Haiku 21*, and was a Snapshot Press eChapbook Awards winner in 2012; "after she leaves" also appears in "THF Haiku," The Haiku Foundation app.

Ash Wednesday—
one farmer out
burning his fields

our father
in the rear-view
mirror

even the arms
of the wheelchair
deer hunter orange

photo of a man
in uniform—
narrow bed

unable to remember
the word for milk —
crows in a snowstorm

the war
on the tv
in the background

closing my journal—
the man next to me
with nothing to read

the garden
after the closing—
someone else's roses

loan
application—
borrowing a pen

after she leaves—
tea stains
on the sympathy card

this familiar church—
some ancient jasper whispers
in a foreign tongue

curve of the river our last fishing trip

        no sex
        many thoughts
        of sex
        many thoughts
        no sex

coyote howling for both of us summer night

yard gate closed—
someone else's
knot

Stewart Baker

Brad Bennett

Claire Everett

Kate S. Godsey

Cara Holman

P M F Johnson

Gregory Longenecker

Jonathan McKeown

Ben Moeller-Gaa

Beverly Acuff Momoi

Polona Oblak

Thomas Powell

Brendan Slater

William Sorlien

Michelle Tennison

Scott Terrill

Julie Warther

Gregory Longenecker

Retired to Poetry

Born 13 May 1947
Los Angeles, California
Currently Resides
Pasadena, California

Since the humanist revolution, finding our place—in space, in time—has become pretty much our full-time occupation. As individuals we are still buffeted by forces we cannot control, but we have more agency in response to them. Longenecker's poems are exactly these sorts of accountings. Whether it is the fallout from experiences in war, in society, in nature, he is asking continuously, What am I in this? Of course there is not always a definitive answer, but sometimes the question is enough.

Credits

forgetting why	*Autumn Deepens*
what	*Modern Haiku* 45.1
gopher hole	*Cattails* 1
all the things	*Ershik* April 2014
dappled sunlight	*deep in the arroyo*
busy	*Acorn* 31
autumn tidepools	*Frogpond* 35.1
crawling	*Mariposa* 26
the dead of night	*Frogpond* 37.2
Mother's things	*ants on the sidewalk: Urban Haiku*
Veteran's Day	*Mariposa* 28
winter	*Bending Reeds*
unsure	*Modern Haiku* 45.3
peeling the orange	Shiki Kukai September 2013
too soon	*tinywords* 13.1

"forgetting why" appeared in *Autumn Deepens* (Yuki Teikei Haiku Society Members' Anthology, 2010); "dappled sunlight" appeared in *deep in the arroyo: Southern California Haiku Study Group Anthology 2012;* "Mother's things" appeared in *ants on the sidewalk: Urban Haiku,* presentation at the 2012 Haiku Pacific Rim Conference, reprised on *Haiku Chronicles,* ed. Alan Pizzarelli & Donna Beaver, 2013; "winter" appeared in *Bending Reeds: Yuki Teikei Haiku Society Anthology,* 2012; "too soon" also appeared in *fear of dancing: The Red Moon Anthology of English-Language Haiku* 2013.

forgetting why
I stepped outside
balmy breeze

what
did they use before . . .
chimney swifts

gopher hole
a part of my life
I don't talk about

all the things
I've done . . .
moving van

dappled sunlight
we make small talk
in the bonsai garden

busy
with their own lives . . .
summer clouds

autumn tidepools . . .
dreams of people
I no longer see

crawling
out of a depression
rock rose

the dead of night
my father wanders
through my dreams

Mother's things
a Hallowe'en photo
no one remembers

Veteran's Day—
accepting some of my wounds
were self-inflicted

winter the rest of the day after we fight

unsure
of the way ahead
fly on the window

peeling the orange our last conversation

too soon to call it love new ice

Stewart Baker

Brad Bennett

Claire Everett

Kate S. Godsey

Cara Holman

P M F Johnson

Gregory Longenecker

Jonathan McKeown

Ben Moeller-Gaa

Beverly Acuff Momoi

Polona Oblak

Thomas Powell

Brendan Slater

William Sorlien

Michelle Tennison

Scott Terrill

Julie Warther

Jonathan McKeown

Owner, Status Flow Plumbing

Birthdate 17 April 1967
Paddington, Sydney, Australia
Currently Resides
Canterbury, Sydney, Australia

Much of McKeown's work, as a first impression, seems to begin overtly in the head. It is as though we are privy to hearing a close observer give voice to speculations. It is the manner in which he proceeds that is unexpectedly affecting. Indeed these poems move consistently from idea toward feeling. It is as if the poet catches himself staring at something, and, realizing why, he then pursues the ramifications of the moment. Subsequent readings also reveal the economy and precision of his language. Some of these poems consists of a mere five or six words, yet seem in no way clipped or telegraphic.

Credits

the smell	unpublished
post-winter	unpublished
morning rush	*A Hundred Gourds* 3.1
still life	*paper wasp* Spring 2013
summer heat	unpublished
gardenia	*Prune Juice* 13
mushroom picking	*Frogpond* 37.1
fungal society	*paper wasp* Spring 2014
thick fog	unpublished
being so	*A Hundred Gourds* 3.2
the image	unpublished
adjusting my spine	*paper wasp* Summer 2013
abandoned quarry	*A Hundred Gourds* 3.1
mossy stone	unpublished
flotsam shore	unpublished

the smell of excitement among packets of seeds

post-winter
blackbird
has spoken

morning rush—
waiting for the honey
to run

still life:
a bowl of fruit
with little stickers

summer heat
the odd-shaped package
on her doorstep

gardenia
she knows
I know

mushroom picking
something about his mother
he never knew

fungal society
the year's last
outing

thick fog
I am asked to listen
for a change

being so the forest can come in

the image
in which I form
the body of our snow-woman

adjusting my spine
on corrugated iron
southern cross

abandoned quarry
the fig tree silently
splitting a rock

mossy stone
the people that built this
forgotten weir

flotsam shore how it all came to this

Stewart Baker

Brad Bennett

Claire Everett

Kate S. Godsey

Cara Holman

P M F Johnson

Gregory Longenecker

Jonathan McKeown

Ben Moeller-Gaa

Beverly Acuff Momoi

Polona Oblak

Thomas Powell

Brendan Slater

William Sorlien

Michelle Tennison

Scott Terrill

Julie Warther

Ben Moeller-Gaa

IT Functional Senior Analyst

Born 16 February 1976
Belleville, Illinois
Currently resides
St. Louis, Missouri

For most people there comes a stage in life when we recognize a certain maturity in ourselves. We own the premises, as it were. An aging parent's instructions can be acquiesced to (if perhaps with an inward smile), and the collisions inherent in a long-term relationship can be negotiated without fear of disaster. The poet's voice throughout the following pages emanates from this grounded place, carrying with it overtones of fulfillment and satisfaction in the responsibilities of being a householder, and being partnered. Yet quite another quality—a concurrent reality, we might say—is glimpsed now and then: a note of innocent, or tentativeness, that belies any drift towards complacency.

Credits

fathers day	*Chrysanthemum* 12
talking over	*World Haiku Review* December 2012
afternoon heat	*Shamrock* 19
evening calm	*Shamrock* 23
twilight	*Shamrock* 20
late evening	*A Hundred Gourds* 2.4
koi pond	*Modern Haiku* 45.1
heat lightning	*Frogpond* 36.3
railroad crossing	*World Haiku Review* December 2012
what she said	*The Heron's Nest* 12.4
sleepless night	*Shamrock* 18
an old argument	*Notes from the Gean* 3.4
after the ice storm	*A Hundred Gourds* 2.3
glowing softly	*World Haiku Review* April 2012
steeping tea	*The Heron's Nest* 15.2

"fathers day" "evening calm" and "an old argument" all appeared in *Blowing on a Hot Soup Spoon* (poor metaphor design, 2014); "afternoon heat" "twilight" "what she said" and "sleepless night" all appeared in *Wasp Shadows* (Folded Word, 2014); "koi pond" appears in *Something Out of Nothing: 75 Haiga by Ion Codrescu* (Red Moon Press, 2015) and *Take-out Window: Haiku Society of America 2014 Member's Anthology* (ed. Gary Hotham, 2014); "an old argument" appears in Never Ending Story (ed. Chen-ou Liu: 6/8/2013).

fathers' day
learning the right way
to snake a drain

talking over living wills
the hum of appliances

afternoon heat
wasp shadows
in the curtains

evening calm
picking cockleburs
from the dog

twilight
the deep glow of coals
      from the grill

late evening
the neighbor's band finally
getting it right

koi pond
removing the weight
of my backpack

heat lightning—
learning when
to hold my tongue

railroad crossing
unable to escape
this conversation

what she said
   driving home
      the sound of blinkers

sleepless night—
the blinking
of radio towers

an old argument
untangling
the christmas lights

after the ice storm
branches heavy
with evening light

glowing softly
in the spotlight
the singer's whiskey

steeping tea
the time it takes to lose a street
to snow

Stewart Baker

Brad Bennett

Claire Everett

Kate S. Godsey

Cara Holman

P M F Johnson

Gregory Longenecker

Jonathan McKeown

Ben Moeller-Gaa

Beverly Acuff Momoi

Polona Oblak

Thomas Powell

Brendan Slater

William Sorlien

Michelle Tennison

Scott Terrill

Julie Warther

Beverly Acuff Momoi

Writer

Born 3 August 1951
Memphis, Tennessee
Currently Resides
Mountain View, California

Art bereft of its tradition has a much reduced ambit. Much of what a poem is depends on other poems that have come before. The cherry blossom image was new only once. Momoi writes with an awareness not only of what we've made of haiku in English, but also what has been made of it in its land of origin. Her images bear the weight of prior usage here, from two cultures, plus the extra frisson her own touch adds. All of which makes the familiar fresh, and grants authority (while enabling our own willing suspension of disbelief) to that which we are encountering for the first time.

Photo credit: Lori Garner.

Credits

year of the dragon	*Acorn* 28
always making	*The Heron's Nest* 14.1
a little fuzzy	*Modern Haiku* 44.3
the pause	*Daily Haiku* Cycle 17
every year	*Blithe Spirit* 24.2
egg moon	*A Hundred Gourds* 2.4
home away	*Daily Haiku* Cycle 17
summer fog	*A Hundred Gourds* 1.1
hurricane	*A Hundred Gourds* 1.1
scorching heat	*Modern Haiku* 42.1
rain clouds	*A Hundred Gourds* 2.1
plucking	*A Hundred Gourds* 1.4
autumn deepens	*Daily Haiku* Cycle 17
black ice	*Modern Haiku* 43.3
spider's silk	*Frogpond* 37.2

"year of the dragon" "always making" "summer fog" "scorching heat" "plucking" and "black ice" all appear in *The Living Haiku Anthology* (ed. Don Baird); "always making" and "a little fuzzy" both appear in *The Sacred in Contemporary Haiku* (ed. Robert Epstein); "always making" also is featured in *Something Out of Nothing: 75 Haiga by Ion Codrescu*; and "a little fuzzy" appears in *Take-out Window: 2014 Haiku Society of America Members' Anthology* (ed. Gary Hotham).

year of the dragon learning to fold my wings inward

always making
something out of nothing
the brilliance of crows

a little fuzzy
about the meaning of grace
scent of apriums

the pause before puddle jumping still plum rains

every year
the same sweet smile
doll festival

egg moon even the dream guide stumbles

home away from home someone else's green mountains

summer fog
all along the coast
new kigo

hurricane now my dream makes sense

scorching heat
the unexpected coolness
of my friend's reply

rain clouds
heavy with waiting
the porch light on

plucking
wild chin hair
autumn chill

autumn deepens my mother's shadow before me

black ice
not seeing your anger
for what it is

spider's silk
the tensile strength
of dreams

Stewart Baker

Brad Bennett

Claire Everett

Kate S. Godsey

Cara Holman

P M F Johnson

Gregory Longenecker

Jonathan McKeown

Ben Moeller-Gaa

Beverly Acuff Momoi

Polona Oblak

Thomas Powell

Brendan Slater

William Sorlien

Michelle Tennison

Scott Terrill

Julie Warther

Polona Oblak

Treasury & Securities Officer

Born 2 March 1963
Ljubljana, Slovenia
Currently Resides
Ljubljana, Slovenia

Our attention can be snagged in a compelling way whenever a writer uses familiar or traditional forms to express unconventional or exploratory ideas. Oblak's themes could be characterized as contemporary and confessional, revealing as they do much about her personal life. Yet her poems are generally couched in straightforward language, and seasonally anchored in a way that lulls and reassures. There may be something of a Trojan Horse strategy at work here, consciously or not: first the familiar, then the unexpected. The pay-off is a conjunction very likely to linger on in the reader's mind.

Credits

river eddies *xxx*
dusty seashell
his hands
if i could
sundog
all that defines
stratus clouds
approaching rain
a dust jacket
after the freight
white lines
unpicked apples
snowflakes
winter thaw
no longer friends

river eddies
the day you asked
me out

dusty seashell
the words he whispered
in my ear

his hands unbutton them mother of pearl

if i could
read your mind
forced paperwhites

sundog what i couldn't say in person

all that defines me babushka dolls

stratus clouds
his slow
recovery

approaching rain
the smell of sauerkraut
lingers on the stairs

a dust jacket
without its book
summer deepens

after the freight train thistledown

white lies
bracken
taller than me

unpicked apples
we promise
to keep in touch

snowflakes all the place she was childless

winter thaw
a bishop missing
from his chess set

no longer friends
the aftertaste
of imported ale

Stewart Baker

Brad Bennett

Claire Everett

Kate S. Godsey

Cara Holman

P M F Johnson

Gregory Longenecker

Jonathan McKeown

Ben Moeller-Gaa

Beverly Acuff Momoi

Polona Oblak

Thomas Powell

Brendan Slater

William Sorlien

Michelle Tennison

Scott Terrill

Julie Warther

Thomas Powell

Potter

Born 26 March 1969
Aberystwyth, Wales
Currently Resides
Gilford, Northern Ireland

Powell's idiosyncratic work exhibits a sure sense of environment and setting, in this case, rural. Within this context, nature is presented as found, or as experienced, without romanticization. Human activities are implied (evidence of peat-cutting, the remains of a sheep) rather than depicted. The prevailing viewpoint is of a poet-as-witness, and apparently based on many years lived in one place. The existence of a parallel world is acknowledged, represented here by the commuter train. For those passengers who chance to see it, do the scarecrow's arms semaphore a reminder of what still underpins the whole?

Credits

spring frost	*A Hundred Gourds* 2.1
how much longer	*A Hundred Gourds* 3.4
spring sun	*Blithe Spirit* 24.3
another year	*Shamrock* 25
budding trees	*Blithe Spirit* 24.2
separating	*A Hundred Gourds* 3.4
black night	*A Hundred Gourds* 2.2
grasshopper	*A Hundred Gourds* 3.1
evening birdsong	*Tinywords* 13.2
commuter train	*A Hundred Gourds* 3.1
as we plunge	*Chrysanthemum* 13
sun-touched gully	*The Heron's Nest* 14.3
vertigo	*A Hundred Gourds* 4.1
peat-stained pool	*Shamrock* 25
clear night sky	unpublished

"grasshopper" "evening birdsong" and "peat-stained pool" will appear in *Clay Moon* (Snapshot Press); "sun-touched gully" was selected Editor's choice for *The Heron's Nest* 14:3 and will appear in *A Dawn of Ghosts* (Snapshot Press).

spring frost . . .
bog birches reach
for two skies

how much longer
along this path . . .
lesser celandine

spring sun skimming the lough with a stone

another year . . .
the rewetting scars
of peat trenches

budding trees
the giddy dog's ear
inside out

                                    rook
                                  rising
      separating   light from shadow

black night . . .
water trickles
through the bog

grasshopper bending light from a blade

evening birdsong
the storm clouds that came
to nothing

commuter train
the outstretched arms
of a scarecrow

as we plunge
deeper into the past
graveyard blackbird

sun-touched gully . . .
the wool and bones
of a passing winter

vertigo deep in the black of the well

peat-stained pool
sunlight fractures
beneath thin ice

clear night sky and how the light echoes

Stewart Baker

Brad Bennett

Claire Everett

Kate S. Godsey

Cara Holman

P M F Johnson

Gregory Longenecker

Jonathan McKeown

Ben Moeller-Gaa

Beverly Acuff Momoi

Polona Oblak

Thomas Powell

Brendan Slater

William Sorlien

Michelle Tennison

Scott Terrill

Julie Warther

Brendan Slater

Unemployed Rat Catcher

Born 10 November 1971
Stoke on Trent, England
Currently Resides
Stoke on Trent, England

"Almost" is never enough but often it's as much as we get, and that with which we must make do. Slater's work is the evidence of his efforts at coping with this reality. His nouns suggest he has known wholeness—how and when and why it might have been a part of his life. But his adjectives and adverbs repeatedly qualify this knowing, making his alignment of desire and actuality proximate. So there is a *justesse* to these circumstances—approaching trust, approaching, love, always approaching. It is this perpetual nearing—this constant motion forward—that is the action of hope, and whose residue are these poems.

Credits

dad and i	*Would that that had never been be*
a spatter	*Notes from the Gean* 2.3
rusty gate	*The Heron's Nest* 2.3
the black cat	*A Hundred Gourds* 12.2
the lie	*Tinywords* 10.1
in and out	*Electronic Poetry Network* 2010
night train	*Acorn* 25
drifting	*Bones* 2
first light	*Notes from the Gean* 2.3
dawn breaks	*Notes from the Gean* 2.4
winter morning	*Notes from the Gean* 2.1
grasping	*Four Virtual Haiku Poets*
snowed-in	*Dream Language*
we share	*Acorn* 25
pewter sky	*Pirene's Fountain* 4.9

"dad and i" also appeared in *Would that that had never been be* (2013); "grasping" also appeared in *Four Virtual Haiku Poets* (ed. Alan Summers & Brendan Slater, 2012); "snowed-in" also appeared in *Dream Language* (ed. Jack Galmitz, 2013).

dad and i
when the sea became the sea

a spatter
of raindrops on the window
abnormal cells

rusty gate
the beaten track
of its swing

the black cat
the neighbour
i almost
almost trust

the lie
i almost tell
bruised ginger

in and out
of sleep
her fingers
turning pages

night train to Amsterdam
our Dutch keeps running
into English

drifting into the colour of same

first light
my last Rizla
taken by the breeze

dawn breaks
between her excuses . . .
ash in my coffee

winter morning
deeper than usual
into the city

grasping
at prayer
moonrise

snowed-in a hyphenated dream

we share
bitter coffee
first light

pewter sky
the litany
of the ocean

Stewart Baker

Brad Bennett

Claire Everett

Kate S. Godsey

Cara Holman

P M F Johnson

Gregory Longenecker

Jonathan McKeown

Ben Moeller-Gaa

Beverly Acuff Momoi

Polona Oblak

Thomas Powell

Brendan Slater

William Sorlien

Michelle Tennison

Scott Terrill

Julie Warther

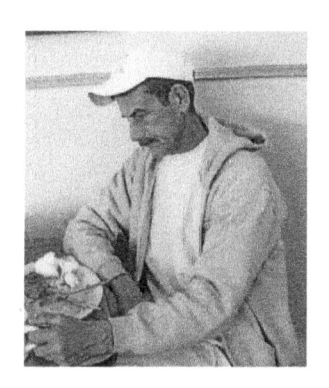

William Sorlien

Construction

Born: 10 October 1956
Kansas City, Missouri
Currently resides
St. Paul, Minnesota

Roland Barthes's fine title *The Empire of Signs* would serve these poems well. These spare images, salvaged seemingly at random, all hold a suggestive weight. But do they cohere? What we surmise from repeated exposure to this work is an eclectic puzzling together of the universe from whatever comes to hand—much as we all do—from a sensibility that at its best is justifiably leery of, and at its worst, paranoid about, the shape of his conclusions, and, consequently, of his own premises.

Credits

a fine spring rain	unpublished
I offer her	unpublished
one glove lost	unpublished
summer clouds	unpublished
Route 66	unpublished
the war	unpublished
afraid of the dark	unpublished
midnight moon	unpublished
footfalls in the rain	unpublished
moving on	unpublished
harvest moon	unpublished
what passes for snow	unpublished
the best lies	unpublished
nothing moves	unpublished
the closest	unpublished

a fine spring rain—
the neighbor's dog
marks all his boundaries

I offer her
my last Pall Mall
blue geese in Fujisawa

one glove lost
the other thrown away—
our spring walk

summer clouds—
not enough paint to hide
the graffiti

Route 66—
a flyspecked whitewash
on the wayside rest

the war
as presented on YouTube—
summer squalls

afraid of the dark,
afraid of the lightning—
calling out the toads

midnight moon—
the rise and fall
of the straw man

footfalls in the rain
so quiet—
my left handedness

moving on
to the next small town
autumn leaves

harvest moon—
halcyon days
in rivertown

what passes for snow—
two trains rumble
in opposite directions

the best lies
the fewest details
cold moon

nothing moves
in the grip of the storm—
still, I lock all my doors

the closest
I'll ever be
to sentimental
a room full of hats

Stewart Baker

Brad Bennett

Claire Everett

Kate S. Godsey

Cara Holman

P M F Johnson

Gregory Longenecker

Jonathan McKeown

Ben Moeller-Gaa

Beverly Acuff Momoi

Polona Oblak

Thomas Powell

Brendan Slater

William Sorlien

Michelle Tennison

Scott Terrill

Julie Warther

Michelle Tennison

Writer

Born 22 April 1963
Cumberland, Maryland
Currently Resides
Blackwood, New Jersey

It is fair to say that haiku has undergone a sea change in the past couple decades. A generation ago Tennison's poems would have had a much more difficult time finding their way into print. For while it is true that we might always have said that our interest here was in describing things as they are, we did so through a filter that largely mitigated the affects that are so compelling here: interiority, sensuality, and, especially, emotional honesty. Such poems seemed to create an imagistic background primarily to foreground the personal drama therein enacted. But in truth it has always been thus. These poems cause us to look, as it were, through the other end of the telescope, and the world we there behold is our world, writ small and in fine detail, and as such eminently available to haiku.

Credits

how many lifetimes	*Modern Haiku* 44.3
pulling the covers	*Modern Haiku* 32.3
just please	*Modern Haiku* 31.2
branches sweeping	*Modern Haiku* 31.2
blossom wind	*Modern Haiku* 45.1
wild roses	*Frogpond* 35.3
hypnagogia	*Frogpond* 37.2
still searching	*Modern Haiku* 45.1
whale song	*Acorn* 32
now that you're gone	*Modern Haiku* 36.1
the inner leaves	*Modern Haiku* 39.1
crows through rain	*Frogpond* 37.3
the last dream	*Modern Haiku* 40.1
probably	*Modern Haiku* 45.3
her eyes	*The Heron's Nest* 13.4

"pulling the covers" also appeared in *The Sacred in Contemporary Haiku* (ed. Robert Epstein, 2014); "just please" also appeared in *Haiku* 2014 (ed. Lee Gurga and Scott Metz, 2014); "blossom wind" also appeared in *big data: The Red Moon Anthology of English-Language Haiku* (ed. Jim Kacian, 2015); "the inner leaves" and "the last dream" both appeared in *Haiku* 21 (ed. Lee Gurga and Scott Metz, 2011); "her eyes" also appeared in *carving darkness: The Red Moon Anthology of English-Language Haiku* (ed. Jim Kacian, 2012).

how many lifetimes
in love with a girl
wisteria

    pulling the covers
        off your shoulders
            my hand passing into moonlight

just please how to forgive spring rain

        branches sweeping
        the darkness of water—
        your breath on my skin

blossom wind
I misread
her intentions

wild roses
you can't tell her
anything

hypnagogia
a rainbow ending
in the ocean

still searching for the god of mourning the sea

whale song
I become
and empty boat

now that you're gone
the blackbirds that were there
all along

the inner leaves
also move
October wind

crows through rain an irrational number

        the last dream—
        held in place
        by cricket song

probably I've done nothing wrong coyotes

her eyes
say yes
fireflies

Stewart Baker

Brad Bennett

Claire Everett

Kate S. Godsey

Cara Holman

P M F Johnson

Gregory Longenecker

Jonathan McKeown

Ben Moeller-Gaa

Beverly Acuff Momoi

Polona Oblak

Thomas Powell

Brendan Slater

William Sorlien

Michelle Tennison

Scott Terrill

Julie Warther

Scott Terrill

Yoga Teacher

Born 11 February 1969
Sale, Victoria, Australia
Currently Resides
Melbourne, Australia

What do these poems mean? Or, to pose the question less naively: what is it they might convey to us, if we could sufficiently open our minds to them? Treading on a thumbtack during the night, that's simple enough—a poem we can relate to without strain, and, perhaps, with relief. But elsewhere we may feel considerably out of our depth, or at best scrabbling for a firm footing in this visceral landscape. What is literal here and what metaphorical? It may be helpful to conceive of the poet as an explorer—of language and association, certainly, but also of the very concept of "meaning." Ultimately we must ask whether, even while often inscrutable, these poems stir us, or provoke, or fascinate, or satisfy.

Credits

truffles	unpublished
deep in the Holocene	*Notes from the Gean* 4.4
as a black crow	unpublished
mangrove and sago	*Southern Humpback*
day clinic	*Southern Humpback*
dreaming	*Notes from the Gean* 4.1
a thumbtack	unpublished
not moving	*Southern Humpback*
a pyramid	unpublished
a crow taps	unpublished
painted by an elephant	unpublished
Dachau	unpublished
Nui Dat	unpublished
cutting of shaping	unpublished
at the end	unpublished

"mangrove and sago," "day clinic," "dreaming" and "not moving" all appear in *Southern Humpback* (Stoke-on-Trent, England: Yet To Be Named Free Press, 2013); "not moving" also appears in *Four Virtual Haiku Poets* (Stoke-on-Trent, England: Yet To Be Named Free Press, 2012).

truffles
in a kingdom of their own
without an anus

deep in the Holocene the softening of a diaphragm

as a black crow I taste the red juice of you

mangrove and sago
sometimes I want to be more
than just a vagina

day clinic
the stigma
of an autumn crocus

dreaming in another language
an oyster dies
beside an oyster

a thumbtack
causes a bleed
in the short summer night

not moving
moving
a fjord and a fjord and a fjord

a pyramid
becomes a mountain
where birds alight

a crow taps on a drain pipe Mexico starts soon

painted by an elephant I leave my name at the door

Dachau
an invisible smell
I know I'm near

Nui Dat
at the back of my tongue
roasted hops

cutting or shaping
he wrote: first bombs
Realism was used too.

at the end of each second a little jiggle

Stewart Baker

Brad Bennett

Claire Everett

Kate S. Godsey

Cara Holman

P M F Johnson

Gregory Longenecker

Jonathan McKeown

Ben Moeller-Gaa

Beverly Acuff Momoi

Polona Oblak

Thomas Powell

Brendan Slater

William Sorlien

Michelle Tennison

Scott Terrill

Julie Warther

Julie Warther

Homemaker

Born 24 June 1969
Dover, Ohio
Currently resides
Dover, Ohio

Warther's haiku are often sharply observant of human motives and behavior (not least the poet's own), with an accompanying ironic tone. This is the case even where the occasion is a solemn or formal one. Indeed, here is precisely the context where the gap between inward thought and outward action can be most interesting, if seldom acknowledged. In contrasting and yet complementary mood, the poet has a sympathetic eye for landscape and the elements. Far from seeking merely to represent them, we find that underlying tensions of dynamics (the shape of a herd, the shifts in a flock of geese) are often the driving interest.

Credits

power suit	*Kaji Aso Contest* 2013
life and death decisions	*Frogpond* 36.3
graveside service	*Frogpond* 34.1
family dinner	*Frogpond* 35.1
before	*European Quarterly Kukai* 6
birding	*Frogpond* 37.3
queen anne's lace	Shukan New York Seikatsu
pasture tree	*The Heron's Nest* 13.4
first warm breeze	*Frogpond* 37.2
untouched wilderness	Klostar Ivanic Contest 2013
first	*Frogpond* 38.1
this side of the pane	Robert Frost Contest 2012
autumn equinox	*The Haiku Calendar* 2014
change in the wind	*Acorn* 30
winter solstice	unpublished

"power suit" won HM in the Kaji Aso Studio International Haiku Contest (2013); "life and death decisions" won HM in the Gerald Brady Senryu Contest (2013); "graveside service" won HM in the Gerald Brady Senryu Contest (2010); "family dinner" also appeared in *Nothing in the Window: The Red Moon Anthology of English-Language Haiku* (ed. Kacian, 2012); "birding" won HM in the Harold G. Henderson Haiku Contest (2014); "pasture tree" also appeared in *carving darkness: The Red Moon Anthology of English-Language Haiku* 2011; "untouched wilderness" won HM in the Klostar Ivanic Haiku Contest in English (2013); "this side of the pane" won First Place in the Robert Frost International Haiku Contest (2012); "change in the wind" also appeared in *Now This: Contemporary Poems of Beginnings, Renewals and Firsts* (ed. Robert Epstein, 2013).

power suit
she pulls
the dangling thread

life and death decisions
a need to feel
the satin lining

graveside service
no one wants to leave
first

family dinner
siblings feed the elephant
in the room

before
and after photos
the dolphins

birding . . .
the unfamiliar path
home

queen anne's lace
the meadow's
white noise

pasture tree
its shade
shapes the herd

first warm breeze
hearing my name
in his voice

untouched wilderness
being alone
with him

first
to break the silence
red-winged blackbird

this side of the pane
the wind nothing
but swaying treetops

autumn equinox
the lead goose drops
to the back of the v

change in the wind
folding over the frayed edges
she begins to mend

winter solstice . . .
a thought draws me to the depths
of the cedar chest